Great Men Are Slain Here

Ernest Hello & Henry de Groux

Léon Bloy

Translated by Richard Robinson

Sunny Lou Publishing Company
Portland, Oregon, USA
http://www.sunnyloupublishing.com

Original Publication Date: 2025 February 28

Translation Copyright © 2025 Richard Robinson
All rights reserved.

ISBN: 978-1-955392-75-4

This translation from French is based on *Ici on assassine les grands hommes*, by Léon Bloy, published by Le Mercure de France, Paris, 1895.

Contents

Translator's Preface

I have always been interested in Ernest Hello and Henry de Groux, as artists and men.

Hello, initially because of his funny last name. (In the case of Bloy, initially because of his mustaches.) Later, as I learned more about Hello, mostly by reading Bloy, but also by reading some of his work, I grew to appreciate him.[1] He is one of a circle, or small pantheon, of French writers and artists whom Bloy counts among his friends or acquaintances (like Barbey d'Aurevilly, Villiers, Verlaine, etc.) whose name often recurs, for one reason or another, throughout Bloy's works.

In the case of Henry de Groux, I learned to appreciate him as a person and artist by reading Bloy's journals; and by, well, looking at his art. (Recently, I had the opportunity to see his *Christ aux outrages* in person, in Avignon. What a treat that was!)

This small book, *Great Men Are Slain Here*, as a biography, does not paint a particularly flattering portrait of Hello as an artist or person (it paints a much less flattering portrait of his wife, "Mama Zoé"). But this does not mean that Bloy loved him any less, – he loved him all the more, quite possibly, because of his failings, so dearly even that he felt he had to set the record straight, in the only way he knew how. Bloy explains his reasons for writing this book in the jour-

---

[1]One of the works read is *Style;* not only read, but translated and published; it is likely that a second will follow. Perhaps one from among the list of titles in chapter 6.

nal entries of *The Ungrateful Beggar*.

As with Bloy, so too with us: we must take the good with the bad when it comes to friends and family – for what other choice do we have, short of rubbing elbows only with saints, tilting at snails, or becoming an anchorite? If we want to get along in this world, we must learn to love people in spite of their failings, and also, sometimes, as the case may be, depending on our Christianity, because of them.

– Richard Robinson, February 25, 2025

Great
Men Are Slain
Here

Chapter One: Heaven and Earth

Heaven and Earth, you cannot scorn him who speaks to you, FOR he is truly weak! ... All I have is my groaning.
– Ernest Hello.

Here it is, ten years now since he was buried, the poor Hello! Nearly ten years. The Catholics did not spare him.

The prodigious Lamenter who wept over their stupidity or their infamy has taken his groaning for a walk in the dark valleys or the luminous valleys of the "sleepers."

The illusion of seeing him again on earth is the exclusive share of a select group of people of Misfortune, welcomed to the terrifying benediction of admiring our Henry de Groux, the painter of carnage, whose physical resemblance to that exhaler of cries is enough to disconcert Death.

Ah! to be sure, they did not miss their mark, those swine of prayer! They took their time, I do not say they did not, but what a triumph in the end!

To be sure, Hello insulted, spat on, ridiculed for thirty years by that entire group of riffraff of the ways of the cross, – it was beautiful! But Hello slain by sorrow, Hello six feet under, Hello adjourned to the Resurrection of the dead, – that was far more beautiful!

With that stick-in-the-mud spoilsport out of
the way, they were free to kiss each other's asses and
lick their lips at ease, to primp their suckers, caress
their trunks, and congratulate their appendages in the
musty, mushroom-infested cupboards of the sacristies
colonized by cockroaches.

They did not anticipate that his books, which
could not be buried with him in the narrow pit where
the vermin of tombs might not have scorned them as
much, would outlive him.

How to guess, when you are one of the legion
of sanctimonious prigs, that works not stamped with
the admiration of sonorous ecclesiastics would one
day manage to escape the well of silence where the
filthy hostility of the so-called Christian newspapers
thought they had engulfed them?

Now, that was precisely what happened.
Hideous hatred was vanquished. The unfortunate Hello's books reappeared.

In the absence of *Style*, which makes works
imperishable, he had the eloquence of an undying un-
bridled enthusiasm, of an ever pathetic imagination,
but, primarily, he had the accent, the elusive accent of
the most marvelous sorrow.

That was all he had, the unfortunate man, and
he knew this quite well, he who wished to be called
the poor of the poor. But it was enough for him to
cease being obscure, to begin shining at a distance of
sixty billion leagues away from the boutiques of de-

votion, and that cried out for vengeance.

Chapter Two: A Relapse of Life

Ernest Hello has quite often looked *at me, [but] I am sure that he has never seen me.* – Charles Buet.

It came, the vengeance, and you will judge for yourself whether it is unsavory. People of "solid piety" are, in general, better informed than fragile people of the sovereign efficacy of ridicule when the intention is to slaughter Greatness.

Ernest Hello, a relapse of Life and Light and, as a consequence, marked for the second time by the exterminating angel that acts among churchwardens, was bound to be struck by the infallible glaive.

It was a matter of writing the semblance of a panegyric, of most profane inanity, capable of disgusting Isaiah himself and casting a shadow on the very constellation of Cygnus.

For such a task, one of those oppressive imbeciles was needed, who are formed in the school of virtue and who appear, it seems, only to assist us conceive of the impenetrable Solitude of God.

That "precious daisy," for the acquisition of which it is recommended that one sell everything, – could it be encountered anywhere else than in Lyon, the Catholic colony of wan Calvin, as everyone knows, where pedanticism and Pharisaic avarice are unparalleled?

I have sometimes offered myself, not without delight, to the unctuous head of a too-well-known polygraph whom Barbey d'Aurevilly was euphemistically pleased to denominate *a frog wearing eyeglasses.*

Ernest Hello's Lyonnais panegyrist appears to be one of his disciples, and it compels me naturally to think about him. But he is only one of his disciples, and so very beneath his master that this latter person, by comparison, stuns me with his majesty. The batrachian suddenly leaps up out of the soil, breaks through the billowy clouds, and hurls packets of thunder...

Little does the name of that insect matter, right? It is even without interest investigating whether his little pamphlet, veritably criminal, was botched with good or bad intentions. It suffices, I think, to know that the basest and most perfidious hatred could not have done a better job at vilifying a great man.

To tell the virtues of the family, of multiple families, the first phrases of the sublime child, the memorable expressions of papas and mamas, the angelic passions of the young man, his marriage plans, the ineffable purity of soul of the fiancés and their union under the watching eyes of seraphim; – things that should have remained in proud obscurity; – to go on and on, finally, about Madame Hello, the divine *Mama Zoé*, in so many pages, great God!... And all that, from beginning to end, in that rheumy form, runny and cold like scrofula, which characterizes the prospectuses of shirtmakers for clergymen or the sac-rilegious instructions of propagation excogitated by some libidinous soutanes.

A little later, – for I confess that I had to pull myself away for several hours from the Holy Book in order to decipher this prattle, – a little later, I say, the author gets carried away in the direction of the abysses of glory.

He strikes a dithyrambic match across his backside and declares to us, among other things, that "Hello, if read and understood, would illuminate the modern mind," that "his glory, *which is that of God*, would have been the good fortune of a century." In passing, he compares him to the Sun. "Hello gives me the impression of someone inhabiting that central and, *at the same time, superior* (!) point in heaven, which, in the world of intelligences, corresponds with the Sun, the celestial center of worlds, the giant focal point that is the synthesis of rays of light before their dispersion in space."

Just try to imagine a man so colossal, a mortal so superhuman, not to be crushed under that avalanche of stupidity!

Even though I do not pass for a writer who has an infinite respect for his readers, I would not dare to take it upon myself to propagate these stupefying cita-tions. My Lyonnais scribbler is not only an idiot, he is also a philosophaster of the disgraceful sort of Protes-tant philosophasters who absolutely must see a meta-physician of his same stable in the lamentable and naïve poet whom he dishonors.

"Thinkers will understand me," he sometimes says knowingly, while he walks on the peas that someone forgot to cook.

Incapable of discovering or suspecting Hello's astonishing *inequality*, whom he calls "a first-rate stylist," (!) at every chance he gets he announces that he will cite something sublime, and it is almost always a platitude.

One needs to be crossbred with Geneva to have a similar sense of smell. Listen to this:

> *"Paul sees a thing from one side; he sees it white.*
>
> *"Peter sees the same thing from another side; he sees it black.*
>
> *"Both are right, both are wrong, for the thing is white on the one side and black on the other.*
>
> *" 'It is white!' Paul cries.*
>
> *" 'It is black!' Peter cries.*
>
> *"And there you have them, two enemies."*

This is from Hello, these several lines of senility, – from the Hello to be kept hidden from all eyes, the Hello to throw into the latrines. And yet! Jocrisse wants them to give a glimpse into the philosophy of his sun, "the great philosophy of a BROAD mind!"

For such is his expression, and such is his wish. Everywhere a man might write *height* or *depth*, he writes *breadth,* victoriously, and he stomps on the vendage.

He needs a broad morality, a broad art, a broad criticism, a broad science, *a broad history*, a broad philosophy, a broad religion, a broad literature. That makes, I believe, eight broad things, just as there are eight Beatitudes in the Sermon on the Mount. It is, all the same, a lot at one time for a short, potbellied, and misshapen man of letters.

These litanies naturally lead us to Mme. Hello who inspired this babbler, and it is about her, it seems to me, that I have something to say.

Chapter Three: A Woman More Bitter than Death

They have killed in me that which is me, that which would have been me. – Ernest Hello dying.

"More fortunate than Jacob," recounts the historian, superabundantly qualified in the preceding paragraphs, "Ernest Hello had better than a stone on which to lay his head, *his head, heavy with the weight of his thoughts*, – he had a heart; but that perhaps would not have been enough for him, – he had an *intelligence*."

That intelligence and that heart, which replaced, in so advantageous a manner, the patriarch's small stone, it belonged to Madame Hello, to the incomparable *Mama Zoé*, as her husband deplorably called her, never realizing the hideous ridiculousness of mimicking Jean-Jacques Rousseau in this way.

This lady, who shared the treasure of her memories and little papers with the profaner and who has become, as her reward, the casqued heroine of an execrable book, would have done better, I think, to employ the last years of her life by asking forgiveness for the crime of having degraded, brought down to her size, and ultimately vilified one of the noblest poets.

I knew her, more than fifteen years ago, when Hello, in the total fervency of his friendship for me, wanted me to contemplate the angel of his life.

She welcomed me with the honey and butter of Emmanuel,[2] while waiting for the not-too-distant moment when she needed to break my heart.

I had no trouble divining that I was in the presence of an inaccessible spouse and a housewife of the highest order who, long time since, must have bored a hole in her husband's chair so that he would not have to get up from his writings.

The poor Hello let himself be washed, combed, dressed from head to toe, like a child. It had gotten to the point where he could no longer put on his trousers without his wife helping him.

One day, when this latter person was ill and the veterinarian[3] who was treating her at the time was delayed in coming, I was the distraught witness of the most inconceivable of scenes. Hello, bumping into everything, *pedibus et manibus offendens*, covering dozens of kilometers in his room, letting out clamors of despair. Seized by a demoniacal rage, frantically invoking all known catastrophes and all unknown ones, he looked like someone dragging the Three Persons of the Trinity by the hair, cursing above all the Redemption, which could only be derisory because his *mama*, immobilized for the last three or four days by arthritis or lumbago, was prevented from doing up his buttons.

---

[2]"Honey and butter: "He shall eat butter and honey, that he may know to refuse the evil, and to choose the good." Isaiah 7:15: (Douay-Rheims).

[3]Original footnote: literally.

It was then that I got a glimpse into the seriousness of that misery. I understood that this indigence of will, the most perfect instance of it that, undoubtedly, could ever be witnessed and which was enough to make a grown man sob with compassion, had to be the chef-d'œuvre of many years of patience. The unfortunate man was literally in pieces.

The extreme nervous susceptibility that he suffered since his childhood had marked him like a too facile prey really for the implacable solicitude of the Minerva he married.

A Christian woman would have undertaken to heal that illness of the will and so completely *effaced* herself that the most attentive biographer would have scarcely noticed her. Mme. Hello did exactly the opposite.

Despotically, she imposed her bourgeois *order* and *balance* on this Benjamin of Ecstasy, who believed, in his simplicity of an innocent, that he had need of both, and he gave her his soul in exchange.

The soul of Hello! the most grandiose and destitute soul that ever existed. At a distance of several years, the memory of it comes back to me like a nightmare. I thought I saw it, this soul of tribulation and desire ruthlessly and continuously forced back into a dark corridor, growing ever more narrow, where the soul would be twisted, contracted, clenched, shriveled like a leaf with infinite anguish.

Ah! It was not a *man* that Mme. Hello needed! What would she have done with one, that prim and proper prude? She needed an *unstable child*, is what she needed, ever more unstable, trembling before her, living through her, *thinking according to her*, believing only in her.[4]

And why is that? Good God! So that the magnificences of her *pot-au-feu* judiciary might one day shine; so that it might be hurled, one day, by a literary runt, into the face of a sniggering world, that she had been a Beatrice or Mentoress of the great man whom she emasculated. *Amariorem morte mulierem*,[5] says Ecclesiastes.

---

[4]Original footnote: Hello's gradual and systematic depression was so surely calculated that until his dying day, on July 14, 1885, he persisted, or *appeared* to persist, in his illusion, while blessing, before dying, a flesh-eating providence that was devouring him. Therein lies the chef-d'œuvre.

"Mama Zoé," he murmured, "you have made me live for thirty years. You have been a mother to me, a good woman, an angel, in the true sense of the word."

One knows that the true sense of the word angel is messenger, *carrier of news*. What did that moribund mean to say, while steeping half in the shadows, half in the light?...

Thirty years! It would have been much better, Madame, not to have let him lived more than ten, provided those ten years of his life were *as a* MAN.

[5]*Amariorem morte mulierem*: Latin for "A woman more bitter than death." Ecclesiastes 7:27 (Douay-Rheims).

Chapter Four: "Lord, I Cannot Bear Your Cross"

My dear monsieur, it is absolutely impossible for us to do what you have asked. Fortunately for us: for if it had not been absolutely impossible, we would have been in a terrible state. We would have seen a thousand relative and secondary impossibilities rise up before us, a thousand reasons to do the thing, and a thousand other reasons not to. The absolute impossibility saves us. – Mme. Ernest Hello to Léon Bloy.

As for myself, I am never mistaken. – The same to the same.

"Lord, I cannot bear your Cross in any other way, but in the light.

"I am so poor that I needed someone to pay for my passage.

"I am not a man, I am an child.

"O God, I can neither act, nor endure, nor wait,

"I am a prodigy of weakness.

"You know that I am too weak to serve you in suffering. That is not my way... In joy, then! Joy!

* * *

"Lord, I am a man of desire; I have that, and I have only that; I offer you my incense, my only wealth.

"Lord, I am too feeble to suffer and die.

* * *

"O God, remember that your hand lit up the stars: give *as you* are, *splendidly, immensely. Overwhelm my desires with the enormity of your gifts. Make me say: God is great, and I did not know it. God is God, and me, – I was sleeping...*

"Ask for nothing from me, give me everything. Act according to our two natures. Pour with both hands. You are Being, and I am nothingness. God, who are, give as you are, without reserve so that I may recognize you. I am someone who is not. I need everything. God, who are everything, give everything to him who is nothing and who needs everything and who hides under the table like the Canaanite woman. You were not being stingy when you cast the stars into the sky....

* * *

"Magnificences, magnificences,... do not celebrate without us!...

"Father, the desire has come from the eternal hills, and my breast has burst.

"Deliver the Alleluia *which will climb toward you, for my heart bursts and can no longer contain itself.*

"... O God, who hold in your hands the breath of creation, receive at last, like a new incense, the supreme cry by which I live and die.

"... The locks are open! The flood-gates are vanquished. Flow, torrents of joy, over the desires that break hearts! Flow, torrents of glory! Alleluia...

* * *

"Heal me, answer my prayers; I am the most miserable creature that has left your hands, and I have nothing else to say... Pity the poor sick child who can no longer go on...

"Lord, as nothingness I have neither right nor power; I am nothing, I can do nothing!...

"Do not be invincible, because *you are God...*

"Father, who take pleasure in yielding, while being the Almighty, in humbling yourself, while being the Most High, in being vanquished, while be-

ing the Glory... Satisfy me, who am meritless, just as you created me from nothing...

* * *

"This immense and indeterminate desire that has always separated me from all *other creatures, this trait of fire that passed between me and the children of my same age,.... this powerlessness to satisfy myself, this inexpressible disgust for the limit, however distant, all that, it is the foundation of the human heart, that is to say, the desire to see the Face of God. His Face, it is his Glory... And his Face, I will see it, on earth, for I have desired it.* Alleluia!

"I will see it, and fall dead; then I will rise again, dressed in his likeness, and then I will speak."

These *prayers*, worthy of the best of *Sagesse* by Verlaine, written far from the eyes of Mme. Hello, and carefully hidden in a mysterious drawer where they were not discovered until after his death, are terrifying.

It must have weighed on the heart of that miserable man, and he must have felt his distress to be able to find such accents! Just reading that shameful and grotesque biography is enough to give one an idea of the chasm of misery into which he had fallen.

What do you think, for example, of the introduction of meat into the contemplative life?

It is a chapter in praise of Mme. Hello, of course, like all the rest, without exception, but more specially written *under her dictation*.

The copyist – having established that "the same hand that merely had to pass over the keys of the piano *to make waves of harmony leap out*, was no less remarkable while roasting a chicken," – ends the poem with the very skilled frying of a beefsteak, *absolutely indispensable* to the blossoming of sublime thoughts, by this simple reflection which I will dare to qualify as virginal:

"The kitchen knife that you see in Mme. Ernest Hello's hands is, for her, one way to sharpen her husband's quill."

One is careful to recall that this wife, "being the guardian of that fine genius, has, in this way, collaborated in his work, and that she has her HIDDEN part to play (!!!) in his inspirations." It is up to us simply to conclude that the ten or fifteen great chapters of *l'Homme* or the two hundred sublime pages scattered here and there were not so much written as belched after excellent meals.

"No one knows what a tender cutlet can do for a man's mind."

And then there is the story of a dog, consoled throughout the night by Mme. Hello, so that its howling might not disturb the sleep of the "dear invalid," a somewhat humiliating anecdote for her husband, which the heroine tirelessly recounts o'er all the earth for nearly twenty years now.

"No one knows what the barking of a dog can do to a man's chefs-d'œuvre."

These things, I think, have no need for very ample commentaries. Ernest Hello could not have done *one single thing* without his wife. She gave him his physical life, intellectual life, and moral life. The author of *l'Homme* owes EVERYTHING to his marriage, and humankind, in its turn, to say nothing of the angelic world, is indebted to *Mama Zoé* for the fructescence of that "fine genius."

There you have it, what was important to announce to several peoples,... that the very personality of the unfortunate man, – already so posthumous before his death, – had irreparably to succumb to the ridicule of like divulgations.

Chapter Five: The Bad Influence of His Wife

First we rape, then we kill, a little later on we maim. –
Marq. DE SADE.

The bad influence [of his wife] so completely dena-
tured Hello that one sometimes wonders whether he
was really meant to be a writer.

The obstinate, invincible absence of *that per-
sonal style* which he strived for, his entire life, is a
confounding thing when one considers, however,
what he produced.

His indigence condemned him to the Sublime,
– in perpetuity. And he could not escape it except
through the cesspools of inanity. When he failed to
reach the sublime, and he often failed, mediocrity itself immediately became for him like a Himalaya. He
fell, like a lightning bolt, to the level of the execrable.
The indescribable misery of his *Contes* is the best
proof of it.

"The force in him," d'Aurevilly wrote, – "an
intellectual power, at times immense, – suddenly de-
volves into weakness." And what a weakness!

"His eunuch style, drubbed into him by an exclusive commerce with frigid pedants and withering
ecclesiastics," I said, in turn, in 1889, "could have de-
veloped into something highly artistic if he had been

able to find enough strength in his reason to seek out another milieu. He never dared, and his punition was to become the author of the *Contes extraordinaires*,[6] where the most emphatic anemia dishonors [the reader] through the obscure adaptations of his religious philosophy to the dramatic realities of life. So much for the lover of art, alas!

"As for the man thirsty for Justice, the millenarian, he did not have to submit to so great a failure, but the indigence of his form sometimes made even the expression of his charity seem pale, so mysterious is human writing!"[7]

Others, of course, should have been able to warn him, but whatever *energy he might have had in his reason* had been so severely compromised that there was nothing left to do, or hope for.

Having been, of course, one of the people he loved the most, I was temerarious enough to try something. But my account was soon settled. *Mama Zoé* made him understand that I was *possessed by the devil*, and the obedience of that disciplined child was so perfect that he abandoned me forever in the blink of an eye.

The last time I saw him, in '81, he was coming towards me, without realizing it, and when he saw me at a distance of about fifty feet, he jumped,

---

[6]Original footnote: One of his greatest poverties was an inability to find titles: *L'Homme* [Man], *Paroles de Dieu* [Words of God], *Contes extraordinaires* [Extraordinary Tales], *Les Plateaux de la Balance* [The Pans of the Balance], etc.

[7]Original footnote: *Un Brelan d'Excommuniés*.

crossed the rue de Sèvres like a bird, and disappeared.

He died four years later without anyone bothering to inform me.

It was one of my greatest sorrows, and it is in this sense that I have said that Mme. Hello broke my heart. I doubt that the memory of this injustice will make the miraculous rosebushes around her deathbed blossom...

Sorrowful man who was consumed by the desire to see the Face of God, but who never noticed the obstacle! Everything that he could have had through his own will, pride, generosity, courage; everything that would have really been *Him*, was sucked out of him with the frightful slowness of vampires.

What God had given to this poor man drowned in tears, – that which was the golden fruit in his enclosed garden, the emolument and ember of his prayer, – that too was snatched from him.

Is it entirely out of the question that Jean Lander[8] could have written *The Path of Life, Daisies in Bloom, Village Tales*,[9] etc., – edifying books wherein Hello's loftiest conceptions was served up to us in caramel?

She served him the medicamentous maxims of the most abject wisdom in return, and it is in this way that we could see, so many times, the contemplative

---

[8]Original footnote: Mme. Hello's pseudonym.

[9]*The Path of Life*...: *le Chemin de la vie* [The Path of Life], *Marguerites en fleurs* [Daisies in Bloom], *Récits villageois* [Village Tales].

man torturing his own genius so that he might align with the sottish formulas that *Mama Zoé* peopled his [Mount] Tabor with. Horrifying transposition!

Mme. Hello's bourgeois *order* was, in reality, the very disorder of hell; balance, common sense, dignity, just measure, and sound reason, the things she browbeat her husband to death with, were ultimately reduced to that final debasement which I see no other way of referring to than as the delirium of advertising.[10]

"Hello," the too-often cited imbecile tells us, "would not have wanted to cry in the desert like John the Baptist."[11] Having become the prey to a sophism of derision, which he would have needed amorously to dissipate with the Archangel's perfumes, and always persuaded that his own *glory* would have been the Glory of God, that gaunt man of Splendor was seen visiting the editorial offices, offering himself, from morning to evening, to the insolence of the swine of the plume, in the hope, always thwarted, of obtaining from them a few lines, a few filthy lines!... He was hoping perhaps for the Kingdom of God from a Lepelletier or a Chincholle!...

Until I saw that, I did not know just how deeply into the depths of ignominy he had sunk.

---

[10]Original footnote: Not even publicity, but vile advertising. He would have joyfully read his name pasted on the walls of urinals.

[11]Original footnote: To be compared to the sottishness mentioned at the start of § III. In the eyes of his historian, *Hello was more fortunate than Jacob* and *would not have wanted to be like Saint John!*... One is kindly reminded that the individual expressing himself in this way is a good Christian.

Chapter Six: Papers

> *I will never be convinced that paternity alone could have saved him. Who knows whether Mme. Hello's* duty, *her unique and profound* duty, *was not to give him children,* no matter how.

What follow, now, are some papers, as perfectly unpublished as old messages can be, buried for years in a box in the far back of a closet.

TO BARBEY D'AUREVILLY.

Kéroman-Lorient (Morbihan).[12]

Monsieur,

I have not received anything from you. Your article – could it be that it was not published? I dare not ask you about it. It is impossible that it be not published. For I departed from you, taking your word of honor with me.

My hand trembles as I write this. Is it possible that you will do as the others have done, and that you will abandon me? To do as the others, that hideous and common thing, that bourgeois crime, to do like the others, to abandon him whom everyone abandons, to

---

[12]Original footnote: All these letters, from 1876 to 1881, are undated. One of the characteristic signs of Hello was that he had no notion of time.

forget the absent one, to forget the ex-
ile, to spit on him who is unarmed and
defenseless, the crime of crimes, the
crime by omission, that for which are
uniquely reserved the anathemas of
the last Judgment:

"For I was hungry, and you gave me
not to eat, etc.";[13] it is absolutely im-
possible for me to associate this cold,
vulgar and hideous thing with your
name, which I love and admire.

You, the great, audacious, and chival-
rous critic, you who are hungry and
thirsty for justice, you the eloquent
and sublime defender of the aban-
doned, you would do as the others!
You, d'Aurevilly!

And I, who, after having written:

The Atheism of the XIXth Century,

Style,

Angela da Foligno,

Rusbrock,

Jeanne de Matel,

The Day of the Lord,

Man,

The Physiognomies of Saints,

---

[13]For I was hungry...: Matthew 25:42.

Words of God,

The Crusader, *etc.*

*I who, after all that, have not one jour-
nal available to me in which to place
an article, I who have been sent pack-
ing to the furthest reaches of the coun-
tryside, I would be abandoned by
d'Aurevilly!*

*No, that cannot be. That is impossible.
I cannot endure the thought. It obsess-
es me during the night. I ask you, in
the Name of God, and at the risk of
your Eternal Salvation, to send me
your article.*

*This letter is for your eyes only; my
hand trembles as I write it.*[14]

– ERNEST HELLO.

TO LÉON BLOY,

Kéroman-Lorient.

My very dear friend,

*Thousands and thousands of thank-
you's to you for your letter. It contains
words that I will never forget.*

---

[14]Original footnote: It is not without utility to observe that this
letter was written after Barbey d'Aurevilly, who was not a "swine
of the quill," had already, partially for compassion and partially
out of veritable admiration, published half a dozen brilliant articles
on the books and person of Ernest Hello.

Since I have been here, my visible and known adversities have taken a turn for the worse, and they have been exceeded by nerve pain and a singular physical suffering whose moral effect is horrible in me. I feel my physical suffering mentally and it destroys something particular in me that it does not destroy in other men.

I insist on this point with you, that you might insist on it as well with God, in your prayers.

I thank you for the presentiments you have expressed regarding me, and regarding yourself in regards to me. It is likely that we are on the verge of an event that will be The Event *rather than an event. This event must be the Advent, or else all is lost. Because it has to do with Salvation, we must pray in the name of Jesus.*

The war that seems to be drawing near is probably the sort of war under which the Event presents itself. That war must needs be something different from ordinary wars. It must needs be what the Apocalypse predicts.

Write to me often, I entreat you. It is possible that I will visit Paris for a short while, in one month. I will reserve a room at the hotel, not having an apartment anymore. How did you manage to get your article published in the Revue?

And the article on me, are you writing it? Your talent is great, and your courage is even greater. You have the courage to anticipate the future.

You do not mention anything to me about M. d'Aurevilly. Where is he now with his Blue Stockings? Does he even remember me? And the abbot T***? Will you be so kind as to tell me what he's up to. Is he in Paris? If you see him, ask him to pray for me.

Dear friend, your letter proves quite clearly that neither time nor space exist for you. You are one of the representatives of Posterity among us.

I advise you above all to pray and to have prayers said for my wife and me.

I embrace you,

— ERNEST HELLO.

Kéroman.

Very dear friend,

For about seven months now, I have had a book at the press, with Palmé. I did not mention it to you. I wanted to surprise you. But as I have no other news to report, it's up to you to give me some. This book of criticism has the title of: The Pans of the Balance.

Perhaps it has appeared without my knowing about it. Perhaps it has been forgotten at the binder Dax, rue de Vaugirard. Would you be so kind as to stop by Palmé's today and find out, and let me know immediately? If the book has come out, you should take a copy for your and d'Aurevilly. Could you find out whether it is at Dax's?

Could you yourself ensure that at least two copies of it are sent to me from Palmé's?

And your articles? I wrote to Paul Féval about them. Paul Féval immediately responded in an amicable letter. He tells me that the insertion of those articles is promised, which he will insist on, and he will pay a visit to Palmé again to that effect.

He adds that he himself is losing influence with Palmé. My own articles no longer appear at all in the Revue.[15]

Given that you are planning to visit Palmé, try to stay calm and talk about your articles. Do not give up. Be gen-

---

[15]Original footnote: *Revue du Monde Catholique.*

tle, but with obstination.

I thank you a thousand times for the magnificent pages that you have sent to me. I have read them to the one person, in Lorient, who can understand them. She was enthusiastic about them. I wait for the notebook that you mentioned. I wait for it impatiently.

As for Events, I am dying with sadness. Nothing! Nothing! Nothing! You no longer speak to me about the asked-for sign. A. M.'s[16] confessor was perfectly right to ask for signs. Does she ask for them? As for myself, I die without them. I suffer physically, I am weak, and I die with the need to obtain something. Ideas are not enough for me; I need events, – evident, palpable, sensible, coarse, but actual events.[17]

Concentrate all your prayers, and all those of your friends, on this necessity for actual events. We absolutely need terrestrial witnesses. For there are water, blood, and fire which give witness on earth. Events! Events! Events! Signs! I am partial to one: yours *over a hundred thousand.* You will succeed!

---

[16]A.M.: Anne-Marie Roulé. For an account of her, albeit fictionalized (but to what degree exactly?), see the character Véronique in *The Desperate Man*.

[17]Original footnote: "I would like a Naturalist miracle," Huysmans said to me one day.

Focus all possible prayers on that same point, and, because I can do no more, obtain that I might SEE today.

Would you be so kind as to provide me immediately with any news on my book? Is it at Palmé's? Is it at the bookbinder's?

A thousand good thoughts. Write to me and send me a journal.

– ERNEST.

Kéroman-Lorient (Morbihan).

Very dear friend,

I want to thank you for having sent me your news. As for myself, I have been suffering a lot, physically and mentally. The heat has made me ill and the Events do not come. I am infinitely more beaten down that you are. Previously, I passed my life in prayer. Then, later, in blasphemy; now in mutism. It is not silence, it is mutism. I am mute, so long as my prayer is not answered. I believe that I suffer much more terribly than you, for I can no longer speak.

So you are going to La Salette, then? I have only one thing to ask of you, and that is to pray for me, that I might SEE

my prayer answered. I am in the abso-
lute necessity of seeing. I am infinitely
more lost than you are, if I do not see
the triumph in this world.

The time is past for me to speak about
it. I do not have the strength to cry. I
submit to death without argument. The
contrast is so terrifying between the
old experiences and the reality that the
latter prevents me from speaking
about the former.

To have hoped for what I have hoped
for, and to be absorbed at every mo-
ment of the day by physical pains and
anxieties of such a nature as to crush
the soul!

There is a state wherein the hopes of
the past appear like ironies, and one is
almost ashamed to think about them.
The setback is so horrible that it can
no longer be expressed in cries. One
hides his head and no longer says any-
thing; for every Word is of the domain,
and within the competence, of Hope.
When hope is lacking, a man is deaf
and mute.

I observe that others can still speak. I
believe that I have a monopoly on infi-
nite weakness. The memory of my an-
cient prayers crushes down on me like
the stone of a tomb. When one has

prayed thus, what to do after that? Where to go? Whom to turn to? I am the one human being in greatest need of help. Make of your Pilgrimage an immense prayer for me. Make it so that I might SEE my prayers answered.

The superior of the missionaries at La Salette, Father Giraud, is considered a saint. Perhaps he will be there, at La Salette, in September. I have never met him. But I have written to him. If you see him, ask him to include me in his prayers.[18]

In general, commend me, with my intentions, to all praying people whom you encounter, even to those who appear insufficient to you and lacking in calibre. The great have not succeeded. Make the little ones pray.

Everyone whom you encounter: Priests, Missionaries, Religious, Pilgrims, even children at the teat, make them pray for me, and for my wife, and with my intentions.

Perhaps your Pilgrimage will procure for you, from that order, some encounter. Look to the payers of those who resemble us the least. Do not

---

[18]Original footnote: I would have been very much on my guard *against* it. The mere sight of these missionaries is enough to crucify Hope.

scorn the lips. Your red-hot iron quill must serve for something. The Scripture that you love so much is written. *The Bible signifies the* Book.

As for my Book, you do not say anything about it. If, by chance, you have not already done so, take it or have it taken. D'Aurevilly has written a very brief article on it, which I greatly thank him for. Give me some news about him. Regards to A. M.

And as for you, very dear friend, bon voyage! Do not renounce your book. In the meantime, write my name in the dust of the great roads that you will pass through, like the name of him who cannot do without seeing and touching what he has asked for and desired!

You will shout my name from the bottom of all the abysses and from the top of all the mountains, like the name of him who absolutely and frantically wants to see, to see, to see on earth what he has asked for!

And you will place my name on all the lips, even the least eloquent, even the most mediocre, so that all, simultaneously, might speak and shout my eternal reclamation!

I have no idea where to send my let-

ters to you. But I entreat you to write to me many times during your trip.

– ERNEST.

Kéroman-Lorient.

I should have written to you many times before, dear and very dear friend! I think of you, and I write to you so seldom. I have suffered greatly since my arrival here. I have had neuralgic pain and have spent many days in terrible discouragement.

The priest of the rue d'Ulm told A. M. just what I had told her myself. A sign is needed. That sign must not be an indifferent thing in itself. It must be important in and of itself, important insofar as the thing it obtains, and important insofar as a sign of other things to come. It must be, at the same time, a satisfaction and a promise of satisfactions!

Now, we are dying of present and devouring needs. So our most present and most devouring needs must be satisfied at once. We need health, success, Evidence. That is the sign we need.

There is a phrase in Scripture that

sums it up nicely: Fac mecum signum
in bonum ut videant qui oderunt me et
confundantur...[19]

*We need a sign that does wonders and
brings the light.*

*What are you up to, dear friend? Are
you writing? What has become of that
book whose subject has grown so
large that no one knows its name or title anymore?*

*I need to see the articles that you
wrote about me in print. The* Corre-
spondant *was so certain a failure that
it is not even a failure. One needs all
the youth of Mme. Zamoyska and all
her innocence to have even considered
it.*

But as for the Revue, *you must culti-
vate [your relationship with] Tr. See
him, be charming. Contain all your in-
dignation. Deploy all your graces.
And if, despite that deployment, the articles do not appear, it may be time for
a booklet. Speak with Mme. Zamoyska
about this thought – that I have need
of that publication and that the bury-
ing of that magnificent work is a crime*

---

[19]*Fac mecum signum*: Latin for "Shew me a token for good: that
they who hate me may see, and be confounded." Psalm 85:17
(Douay-Rheims).

and a misfortune that weighs on me. [20]

Would you not do well to see the priest on rue d'Ulm yourself? Tell me everything that you are up to and, if possible, everything you think, everything you hear in the air, all the sounds that pass over your head and around you.

M. d'Aurevilly, has he celebrated Easter? Remember me to him. I think about A. M. Be prudent with her in every sort of way and, whatever she says, whether good or bad, write it down for me. I would like to have the pages that you write or that you think to write.

Thousands and thousands of good feelings,

– ERNEST.

Kéroman-Lorient (Morbihan)

Dear friend,

Your letter has made a profound impression on me. Deeply suffering and very sorrowful myself, I would have postponed my response to you until a

---

[20]Original footnote: That magnificent work was an undigestible dithyramb of twelve or fourteen hundred lines, several scraps of which were scarcely useable in the second chapter of *Brelan D'Excommuniés*, published ten years later, after I had become a writer, for my eternal damnation.

little later, if I did not think that perhaps you were waiting for a word from me, and that perhaps a silence, even a short one, would seem like a cold shoulder.

I will not try to describe to you the horror that our situation causes me. That terrible disappointment leaves me speechless, and anything I could say would come up short.

My cries are dead for their excesses and would seem insignificant to me now compared to the situation they tried to express.

I will write to you more at length. I will only mention a couple of things to you today.

Here is the first: Do not let the desire for great things make you neglect the small ones. Do not look down on your articles written about me, Take care of your affairs. Do not interrupt your book.

I have just written to Paul Féval to remind him about your articles with Palmé. If you cannot see Palmé, nurture your relationship with Paul Féval and talk to him. Attend to your affairs, day after day, and do not neglect any of them. You should habituate yourself to gentleness and be capable of seeing

Palmé. You have perhaps said all your prayers except that one. Who knows if by chance that one might not be the best one?

Be gentle, and with that gentleness say a prayer for us all.

And those are the small things. You must do them.[21]

As for the great things, given that nobody can do them, you must tell me about them. All that you think and all that A. M. says to you of the most extraordinary kind, things too strange to endure, even by me, those are things I long for.

Recount *to me the most enormous things. And* do *the simplest things, the smallest, you must.[22]*

And pray with all your strength for my health, which is pitiable.

Goodbye, dear friend, write back again very quickly with any news. And tell me things too astonishing to be supported.

— ERNEST.

---

[21]Original footnote: Platitudes, obviously written by the poor great man under dictation by his wife. The *good* Mme. Hello was a firm believer in "small things."

[22]Original footnote: Again!

Chapter Seven: Henry de Groux

In similitudinem aquilæ volantis cum impetu.[23] –
Deuteronomy 28.

Now on to you, my very dear Henry de Groux, prodigious Double of the great Hello, you who frightened me one day with that terrible resemblance, and whom I love, *above all for that reason*, even though you are, perhaps, the greatest artist in the world.

It is for you, the ardent visionary of the *Christ aux Outrages*,[24] that this work was done, not without great fatigue, this work of cleansing the face of sorrow and splendor, – your face, – which others tried to cover with filth.

Who better than you, then, o very dear friend, could understand me? There are days, you have often noticed them, when I barely know who you are, when I hesitate before uttering your name, so identical are you in my eyes to that Ignored Man, – whom the foolishness or vanity of those who killed him profanes even today, in the grave.

Your Menaechmus could not contemplate God except in a flurry of glory. Entrusted with a mission, I want

---

[23]*In similtudinem...*: Latin for "Like an eagle that flyeth swiftly." Deuteronomy 28:49 (Douay-Rheims).

[24]*Christ aux outrages*: For more on this painting, and Henry de Groux, see *The Ungrateful Beggar*, Sunny Lou Publishing, 2025.

to suppose, for the fulfillment of his work, you could not have shown us this same God except in the bloody tourbillion of ignominies. Is this not exactly the same vision in the Absolute?

But it seems to me that you have received the better share. Blood is stronger than the Light, and you know that the Death of Christ blotted out the sun.

Would it not be sublime if the unfortunate Hello, who so debased his heart in his insane desire to enthrall men's attention, would have been mysteriously condemned to triumph only *in you* who carry your soul so high and for whom the approval of the multitude is the perfect opprobrium?

Other Books by the Publisher

Fanchette's Pretty Little Foot by Restif de la Bretonne

Je M'Accuse... by Léon Bloy

My Hospitals & My Prisons by Paul Verlaine

Salvation Through the Jews by Léon Bloy

Words of a Demolitions Contractor by Léon Bloy

Cellulely by Paul Verlaine

Ecclesiastical Laurels by Jacques Rochette de la Morlière

Flowers of Bitumen by Émile Goudeau

Songs for Her & Odes in Her Honor by Paul Verlaine

On Huysmans' Tomb by Léon Bloy

Ten Years a Bohemian by Émile Goudeau

The Soul of Napoleon by Léon Bloy

Blood of the Poor by Léon Bloy

Joan of Arc and Germany by Léon Bloy

A Platonic Love by Paul Alexis

The Revealer of the Globe: Christopher Columbus & His Future Beatification (Part One) by Léon Bloy

An Immodest Proposal by Dr. Helmut Schleppend

The Pornographer by Restif de la Bretonne

Style (Theory and History) by Ernest Hello

Enamels and Cameos by Théophile Gautier

Four Years of Captivity in Cochons-sur-Marne: 1900-1904 by Léon Bloy

Dark Minerva: Prolegomena: The Moral Construction of Dante's Divine Comedy by Giovanni Pascoli

What is Fascism: Discourses and Polemics by Giovanni Gentile

The Desperate Man by Léon Bloy

Meditations of a Solitary in 1916 by Léon Bloy

The Ride of Yeldis & Other Poems by Francis Vielé-Griffin

Silvie & The Chimeras by Gérard de Nerval

Italian Nationalism by Enrico Corradini

A Silver-Grey Death and *Drowning* by Yu Dafu

Doctrines of Hatred, Part I: Anti-Semitism by Anatole Leroy-Beaulieu

Rhymes of Joy by Théodore Hannon

Windows and Doors by Richard Robinson

The Perverted Peasant by Restif de la Bretonne

Early Poetry by Auguste de Villiers de l'Isle-Adam

Antisthenes: The Founder of Cynicism by Charles Chappuis

The Ungrateful Beggar by Léon Bloy

.

www.ingramcontent.com/pod-product-compliance
Lightning Source LLC
Chambersburg PA
CBHW030519130626
46549CB00007B/3067